STRAIGHT ON 'TIL MORNING

Trish Harnetiaux

BROADWAY PLAY PUBLISHING INC
224 E 62nd St, NY, NY 10065
www.broadwayplaypub.com
info@broadwayplaypub.com

STRAIGHT ON 'TIL MORNING
© Copyright 2006 by Trish Harnetiaux

Cover photo by Jude Domski

First printing: May 2006
This printing: November 2015
I S B N: 978-0-88145-308-9

Book design: Marie Donovan
Word processing: Microsoft Word
Typographic controls: Ventura Publisher
Typeface: Palatino
Printed and bound in the U S A

STRAIGHT ON 'TIL MORNING was originally
produced by the 78th Street Theater Lab (Eric
Nightengale, Artistic Director; Mark Zeller and Dana
Zeller-Alexis, Producing Directors; Ruth Nightengale,
General Manager) and Morning Line Productions
(Co-Founders Jude Domski and Trish Harnetiaux) in
New York City, opening on 3 September 2004. The cast
and creative contributors were:

PETER .... Michael Colby Jones
NICO .... Jason Griffin
FRIENDLY ....Maurice Edwards
MOIRA .... Kate Turnbull
PRICE .... David L Carson
ISABELE .... Corey Tazmania Stieb
HOARD .... Edward Furs

Director .... Jude Domski
Costume design .... Rabiah Troncellitti
Lighting design .... Steve O'Shea
Sound design .... Owen O'Malley
Set design .... Sarah Pearline
Dramaturg .... Jude Domski
Assistant director .... Heidi Handelsman
Stage manager .... Eve Gibson

CHARACTERS & SETTING

PETER, *twenties, early thirties*
PRICE, *forties*
MOIRA, *twenties*
ISABELE, *twenties*
HOARD, *fifties*
FRIENDLY, *sixties*
NICO, *twenties*

Time: The Now

Place: Brooklyn

THANKS

Jude Domski, Eric & Ruth Nightengale of the 78th
Street Theater Lab, Ada Limón, Heather Grossmann,
Laura Davison, Jason Pendergraft, Cindy Price, and
Bryan & Sue Ann Harnetiaux.

To the actors from the original production, and to the
actors that were part of the development process: Jason
Pendergraft, Jen Donlin, Rachel Sledd, Joel Israel, Lia
Aprile, Stephanie Dodd, Bill Green, Jason Griffin,
Wilson Hall, Lee Coco, Timothy Reynolds and Toby
Wherry.

The good people of Kirriemuir for keeping the bars
open late, the lady at J M Barrie's house for letting
us touch his stuff, Phyllis for championing the pool
forever, Patty Vech at The Turkey's Nest 'cause he's the
real deal, the ladies of Ms Elle's for keeping us in wine
& cherry dishes and especially to all the Italians, Polish,
Latinos and Hasids who got here first.

SOME NOTES

STRAIGHT ON 'TIL MORNING is *inspired by*—
not an adaptation of—the story of Peter Pan, the life
of J M Barrie and the youth Mecca of Williamsburg,
Brooklyn, a diverse neighborhood undergoing rapid
gentrification. So caution, do not look for the allegorical
counterparts for all you know about Peter Pan—
it was but a point of departure. STRAIGHT ON 'TIL
MORNING smashes up bits of everything, and adheres
to no rulebook.

Music is integral to any production. Peter is an A & R
guy for an indie rock label and the music chosen should
reflect his cutting edge sensibility. No specific songs
or bands are called out in the script because the music
must be new or rising musicians on the indie scene at
the time of production. The song chosen as the last song
must be the best song ever written.

The action of the play takes place over the course of one
day.

This play should be performed with no intermission
(because no one really *likes* intermission.)

All children, except one, grow up.
J M Barrie, *Peter Pan*

Prologue

(5 A M. The tower overlooking the abandoned pool. PETER, *carrying a large Styrofoam to-go cup of beer from the bar, enters with* NICO *close behind. They stop and look out over the pool.* FRIENDLY *enters.)*

PETER: Behold the kingdom.

FRIENDLY: My god.

NICO: Incredible, isn't she.

FRIENDLY: It's—

PETER: Breathtaking.

FRIENDLY: Heartbreakin'.

NICO: Twenty years, huh?

FRIENDLY: Twenty-two.

NICO: Wild.

FRIENDLY: Used to be. It was different then.

PETER: It's better now.

NICO: How so?

FRIENDLY: It had water in it then.

NICO: Right.

FRIENDLY: God, the weeds, graffiti, and Jesus— *(Pointing across the pool, a shadow movement has caught his eye.)* What the hell is that?

PETER: Don't worry—close your eyes.

*(*NICO *dutifully closes his eyes.)*

FRIENDLY: Close my eyes?

(Keeping one half-open on PETER.*)*

PETER: Trust me.

NICO: Trust him.

PETER: Squeeze them shut...and you see the lagoon... and once you see that, you'll see the prize, the *money*— you'll see the Mermaids.

FRIENDLY: Mermaids?

NICO: I can't quite see them...

PETER: Lounging in the moonlight. Hold still...a minute longer—you can hear them singing. That my friends is the closest thing to heaven there is.

FRIENDLY: *(Scoffing)* I hear nothin'. *(Opens his eyes, breaking* PETER*'s spell.)*

NICO: Friendly—what was it like? In it's prime?

PETER: It's in its prime.

FRIENDLY: It was immaculate. People everywhere maintaining it, cleaning it. People'd line up around the block to get in. The water sparkled—it was like a picture book. No joke.

NICO: I bet the whole neighborhood could fit in here.

FRIENDLY: More. People'd come from everywhere. We'd spend the whole day here for a dime. It was the center of the neighborhood. Look at this. Now it's an eyesore, a *problem*. Ironical, it being built during the depression.

NICO: Why?

FRIENDLY: 'Cause it's depressin' now. Don't know why I let you talk me into coming—

PETER: Look at this—it's *beautiful*. Me, Nico, Isabele, Jack and everyone else I've brought in here love it and let it's grandness sweep over us. It's run down and forgotten about and feels like it knows something.

NICO: Something we don't.

PETER: The energy—it's authentic.

FRIENDLY: Authentic?

PETER: Real.

NICO: The real deal.

PETER: Pure.

NICO: You can feel the ghosts.

FRIENDLY: Uncle Doc used to say some places had "the atmosphere of generations."

NICO: Like Coney Island!

FRIENDLY: *(Pointing across the pool)* See those grates over there, next to the islands on the bottom of the pool?

NICO: Yeah.

FRIENDLY: *(Chuckling)* Kids used to swim to the bottom, get their fingers stuck.

NICO: That's what happened to Hoard's hand, right?

FRIENDLY: Jeez—lucky.

PETER: Yeah—lucky.

FRIENDLY: He was saved by Mary Ann Carter Daome's sister. She reached down and lit-er-a-lly pulled him up by his hair. Big girl, strong. Not so lucky for the hand.

NICO: That'd be it for me, I wouldn't go back in. You ever go at night, sneak in?

FRIENDLY: Me? No. Some kid's would. That's when most of the drownings would happen.

PETER: Learn to fucking swim. I'm going to fill this place with rock 'n roll that's ready to explode—riffs, harmonies, rhythms.

FRIENDLY: Heard you stood up to Hoard in front of the Community Board.

NICO: Peter was a goddamn hero last night.

FRIENDLY: People don't usually challenge him.

PETER: I think it's in the bag, we got it.

NICO: "The Bands Over The Bridge Festival."

PETER: Everyone'd come.

NICO: The feel of the Siren.

PETER: We'll have the Blogs play.

NICO: The Snatch Monkeys.

PETER: Jolly Roger headlining.

NICO: Madness.

PETER: An all-night party—all local, hand-picked.

NICO: Oh, god, perfect. They'd play in the deep-end, where the deep-end was -

FRIENDLY: Make sure they all stop by the bar and it's fine by me!

PETER: "Sponsored by Ship's Mast."

NICO: "Ship's Mast Presents."

FRIENDLY: *(Starting to smile)* I like it. Couple years ago, they had a little money earmarked for this place.

NICO: To re-open it?

FRIENDLY: Meetin' to decide was supposed to be September 17th. 2001.

NICO: So it never happened.

FRIENDLY: Never will.

PETER: You're bringing me down, man.

FRIENDLY: We're last on the list.

PETER: *They wouldn't have to do anything.* Raw works.

(It's starting to get a bit lighter outside.)

PETER: Sun's creeping up.

FRIENDLY: Bedtime. This isn't for me anymore.

PETER: I'm going to wait on the sunrise.

NICO: Me too.

FRIENDLY: Well thanks for bringing an old neighborhood guy into your world.

NICO: Our world.

PETER: Remember to cover the hole in the fence.

FRIENDLY: Alright, 'night. Be careful.

PETER: Nothing to be careful of.

NICO: See ya.

(FRIENDLY exits. PETER and NICO sit looking out over the pool.)

NICO: A toast.

PETER: A toast.

NICO: To the pool.

PETER: *(He slowly closes his eyes.)* To the pool.

NICO: Peter—

PETER: Shhhh, Nico, listen man.

NICO: What?

(PETER puts oh his aviator sunglasses and takes a sip of beer as the light grows brighter and brighter.)

PETER: It's the Mermaids, they're singing.

Scene I

(12 noon. PETER's *Loft.* PETER *appears on the fire escape outside the huge window peering into his loft. He watches* MOIRA, *asleep on the bed, for a moment then opens the window and slips in. The space is sparse. A bed, scattered clothes, music magazine's and cd's spread throughout.* PETER *has not slept and is jumpy, pacing and wired. He has his headphones around his neck and is talking to himself.* MOIRA *is beginning to wake and is extremely hung-over.)*

PETER: ...and I'll kill myself in the end. I know that much. Right before everything starts to shut down and sag. Before the first wrinkle or gray hair— I'll throw myself in front of a train.

*(*MOIRA *makes a noise.)*

PETER: A perfect, tragic end. I'll pick the date! Something definite, controllable. It'll be an adventure. Spring? May 19th... No—April 22nd...

MOIRA: Peter.

PETER: I see it.

MOIRA: Lovely.

PETER: I could die in battle. *(He is searching the loft, looking for his hat.)*

MOIRA: Come snuggle with me.

PETER: Or be hit by a car—

MOIRA: My head is spinning.

PETER: Saving some kid. A hero.

MOIRA: We drank every beer in Brooklyn last night.

PETER: Where's my hat?

MOIRA: Does the party ever stop here?

PETER: Have you seen my goddamn hat? Moira— my hat? It's gotta be somewhere—

MOIRA: *(Finding his hat in the bed.)* Here.

PETER: One girl is worth twenty boys.

MOIRA: *(Feeling the momentary panic of having slept too late.)* God, it's beautiful out.

PETER: *(Hearing the music of Jolly Roger in his head.)* I can't get that goddamn music outta my head, I love it. I can taste it.

MOIRA: That was so much fun, hanging out with all those bands last night.

(PETER doesn't respond to her, he is caught up in the music. MOIRA throws a pillow at him to get his attention.)

MOIRA: Peter?

PETER: Do you challenge me with this pillow?

MOIRA: No, no pillow fight, please.

(They have a pillow fight. PETER's cell phone rings. It is an annoying ring, some whiny indie song. He glances at the number and doesn't answer it.)

PETER: Fuck.

MOIRA: What?

PETER: The time. What time is it?

MOIRA: Noon. My god, is that possible?

PETER: Fuck.

MOIRA: What?

PETER: Isabele's at Exxon Cafe, I promised—

MOIRA: We have plans all day.

PETER: She's leaving tomorrow for the tour. I gotta return some book.

MOIRA: You're going to show me where that guy is off Lorimer.

PETER: What guy?

MOIRA: The cheese. That guy that smokes his own mozzarella. The old Italian guy with the long whiskers—

PETER: That's a chick.

MOIRA: I want to get it for dinner.

PETER: It's not gonna take me that long. You know what you should do—

MOIRA: What.

PETER: Check out that yoga place—Blow Yoga.

MOIRA: Stay here.

PETER: I'll be back by the time your done. *(Going to her gently)*

MOIRA: Pleeeeeaaaasse.

PETER: We'll sit and you can tell me all about the wild, wild west.

MOIRA: If you're lucky.

PETER: Super fuckin' lucky.

MOIRA: You love my stories—

PETER: That I do.

(Starts kissing her neck, she is succumbing.)

MOIRA: Which is your favorite.

PETER: You know my favorite.

MOIRA: Porthos.

PETER: The rattle of the battle. Well—come on—please, please, please—

MOIRA: *(A master storyteller)* Porthos the salmon was born quite forlorn, and swam from his river of birth. He had quite a nose for the river he chose was a thrill for all it was worth. The river has danger with many a stranger—there are bears around every bend. But Porthos did know to follow the flow—not mistaking a foe for a friend. He befriended a trout with razzle and dazzle that he swam with for part of the way. But the trout was too tricky (and Porthos was picky) —their rapport lasting only one day. He followed his notion—was "off to the ocean!" There'd be whales and sea lions to rattle. And he polished his swiggle and slicked back his wiggle—prepared for the thrill of the battle. *(She stops.)*

PETER: And? And? Oh—come on—

MOIRA: You get the rest when you come home.

PETER: *(Starts humming a rock song, distracting himself.)* Shit—that band is *it*.

MOIRA: Those burlesque girls with the doves and the hula hoops?

PETER: No, fuck them, Jolly Roger.

MOIRA: I think it's funny someone pays you to see bands.

PETER: *Find*. They pay me to *find* bands.

MOIRA: Can you find me one?

PETER: A band?

MOIRA: For us...

(There is a knock on the door.)

PETER: Fuck.

MOIRA: Who's that?

(She starts frantically straightening up. PETER looks through the peephole and freezes.)

PETER: Oh god.

MOIRA: Is that *her*?

(MOIRA continue picking up. PETER is frozen in place.)
Well?

PETER: *(Whispering)* Well what?

MOIRA: Aren't you going to get it?

(PETER slowly unlocks the door and opens it. A well dressed, if not severely academic looking PRICE enters.)

PETER: Hi.

PRICE: Peter.

(There is an awkward moment where they are not sure how to greet each other.)

PETER: My God—

PRICE: Hard to believe—

PETER: Holy shit—

PRICE: Good to see you—

PETER: It's been—

PRICE: Years. I took the train down this morning.

(They just stare at each other.)

MOIRA: Hi!

PETER: Oh, Moira—Moira—Price.

MOIRA: I just woke up, sorry.

PRICE: No, I'm sorry. I thought, well, it's early afternoon—

PETER: Price is, uh, Price is my uncle.

MOIRA: I didn't know you had an un—

PETER: *(Cutting her off)* How'd you find me?

PRICE: I saw your name in the paper last year.

PETER: Which one—did everyone see it?

PRICE: Something to do with a concert—

PETER: The Siren.

MOIRA: Peter had some bands playing—

PRICE: I assumed you were still living down here.

PETER: Yeah—forget the Siren—I'm launching this new festival. In the pool.

PRICE: The pool?

MOIRA: It's this abandoned neighborhood playground of sorts.

PETER: *(Looking for a way out)* Isabele!

MOIRA: God.

PRICE: I've come at a bad time.

PETER: No, no it's good to see you.

MOIRA: You've come at a perfect time.

PRICE: Are you going somewhere?

PETER: No, I just have to meet a friend and drop something off real quick.

PRICE: So you're going somewhere.

PETER: Fast, I'm fast. *(To* PRICE*)* I wouldn't even go, it's a long story.

MOIRA: It's not long.

PRICE: If I remember correctly, with Peter, they are usually long and often involve extreme forces of good and evil.

MOIRA: It's not even a story.

PETER: You've always been the storyteller Price.

MOIRA: I thought I was.

PETER: *(Grabbing his jacket)* Right. You both are—you should get along great. Five minutes. See ya in a sec. *(He exits.)*

PRICE: I'm sorry I didn't call first.

MOIRA: No, it's fine.

PRICE: I should have called. I thought it best just to come.

MOIRA: Of course. You're family.

PRICE: It's been years since I've seen him.

MOIRA: How long?

PRICE: A decade. At least.

MOIRA: Huh. So you live...

PRICE: In Connecticut.

MOIRA: It's good to meet someone that's known Peter, you know, his whole life.

PRICE: Does he talk about his family much? Home?

MOIRA: No... There's so much going on here.

PRICE: Of course.

MOIRA: Peter's...what's a good word...hard to pin down?

PRICE: Sounds right.

MOIRA: There's something charming about it. He has such a wild imagination and passion.

PRICE: Yes. How's he doing?

MOIRA: Great. He's mad about music. He works at Region, this indie label. He's got this absurdly fun job of finding new, cool bands. What was he like, you know, growing up?

PRICE: Slippery.

MOIRA: Slippery?

PRICE: *(Laughing)* Like you said, hard to pin down. He'd hide in the trees, wouldn't come out. Everyone would be at dinner and Peter would be in the woods content to live in some tree house he built.

MOIRA: *(Cautiously)* And Michael?

PRICE: Michael?

MOIRA: Peter's only mentioned him once, briefly. I'd found a photo of him tucked under the mattress.

PRICE: Michael was...delicate. Needed attention. He was fueled by the summers at Black Lake—

MOIRA: What's Black Lake?

PRICE: Peter's never told you?

MOIRA: No.

PRICE: It was our family's summer place. Magical. Peter, Michael and I played the woods. I was the orchestrator and they the symphony. The lake becoming a South Sea Lagoon. We were ship wrecked. Fighting off tigers armed only with a bow and arrow. We were inseparable. We lived in "The Now".

MOIRA: The now?

PRICE: We had "The Now". Michael actually had a cat that he named "The Now".

MOIRA: As in the present?

PRICE: What else was there.

MOIRA: "The Now"... Sounds very—French.

PRICE: *(Laughing)* Michael would run around the woods yelling, "Come here The Now! Meow The Now"

MOIRA: So, what is it that you do?

PRICE: Do I do?

MOIRA: You know, in "The Now."

PRICE: That's like asking how old you are.

MOIRA: *(Laughing)* It is not.

PRICE: I teach at a small college. My book primarily, Narcissus, and a smattering of Lit 101 classes.

MOIRA: Narcissus...he starves to death staring at his reflection, right?

PRICE: That's one version, yes.

MOIRA: Are their others?

PRICE: Many. There are variations of the myth, it's evolved over time with society. It's the thought behind the story that interests me, the true-self, the false-self, what happens when you live an unauthentic life.

MOIRA: Unauthentic?

PRICE: How when one is untrue to one's self one lives an inferior existence.

MOIRA: What's your version of the myth?

PRICE: He drowns. Sinks into the water to be closer to himself.

MOIRA: *(Her hang-over is starting to come back.)* Chilling.

PRICE: I don't mean to sound so...depressing.

MOIRA: No worries. *(She puts on her flip flops, holding her head slightly.)* Are you hungry? Let's have brunch. There's this ridiculous little place I've been wanting to

check out—GKAR. *(Pronounced "R")* It's spelled
G-K-A-R. The G and K are silent.

PRICE: Sounds, ah, interesting.

MOIRA: It's also a notary. In case you need to,
you know, notarize something.

PRICE: Do you think Peter will be long?

MOIRA: It's hard to tell. I'll give him a call.

PRICE: Who was he meeting?

MOIRA: Isabele. She's a waify, needy little sprite that
never wears a coat. He'll find us, don't worry.

Scene II

(1 P M. Ship's Mast. FRIENDLY *is behind the bar talking to a
customer.*

FRIENDLY: That place? Down on Kent? Used to be New
York's first all black topless bar. They're tryin' to rent
it out as an apartment now. They'll rent out anythin' at
this point. Can only imagine what sort of stories they're
spinnin' to jack up the price,just talk to Hoard, he owns
it. He's probably sayin' Harriet Tubman herself used to
woo the crowds. Funny thing is you dig two feet down
in the backyard and strike oil—and not the fancy Texas
kind. Biggest spill ever back in the seventies—millions
and millions of gallons just oozing below the surface.
No Joke.
   Hoard? He's got his Real Estate office over on
Graham, considers himself a "developer" now,
whatever that means. He needs to take it easy, starting
to throw around a bunch of ten dollar words, getting
a bit hard on the ears if you know what I mean.
   Yeah, I'm on top of all that pool talk too. Well Hoard's
got a forty-year grudge festerin' there, his hand and all.

He wants to put up some sorta skyscraper. But the kids—they want to turn it into some kind of concert place, some kind of a *festa*. I'm not taking sides.
It used to be immaculate. Tended to your every need. You needed a towel? They had towels. And they were handed to you by a pretty lady. Another era. *Che Peccato.*

Yeah, it's been changin'. Still changin' some say. They all started movin' in about ten, fifteen years ago. Word was the village had spread as far east as it could get and prices were driving them artists over the bridge. I don't mind too much, shoved the Hasids down some which they're not happy about, concentrated most of the Poles nicely past the park, didn't bother us Italians really, we've pretty much kept our hold on the immediate area, and them Latins always had their Southside. More people like yourself though coming in asking questions all the time.

Last few years has breathed some new life in this place. I am now a condo owner in the sunny state of Florida. No Joke.

We don't o-ffici-ally open for another hour, but can I buy ya a drink?

Scene III

(2 P M. The bench in the park near Exxon Cafe. ISABELE *is sitting there waiting. She's got that waify-indie-token-chick-bass-player look.* PETER *enters, late.)*

PETER: So listen, I can't have brunch with you.

ISABELE: Me? I'm well, thanks for asking.

PETER: I mean it.

ISABELE: I've been waiting here for a year. It's two. Pick up your fuckin' phone.

PETER: She's pissed.

ISABELE: Leave then.

PETER: I shouldn't even be here.

ISABELE: Christ, Peter.

PETER: *(Handing her a worn copy of* A Heartbreaking Work of Staggering Genius.*)* Here's your book. God, I've been up all night—

ISABELE: *(Thrilled)* So have I! Why do you think I'm dressed like this. It was madness—we had the most fucked up gig. Hey—where were you—

PETER: "Where were you?"

ISABELE: The show—

PETER: I totally forgot. Sorry.

ISABELE: You still haven't seen us play.

PETER: Next time, I absolutely promise.

ISABELE: That's such bullshit.

PETER: So what happened?

ISABELE: F-D-N-Y. God! It was so frustrating. We went on after this feathered little wench that sang these pansy-ass candyland vocals—

PETER: Was she hot?

ISABELE: Excuse me?

PETER: I think I know who your talking about— headband, Indian, really cool—

ISABELE: *Um, no.* Anyway, we go on right after them, I mean people are ready to hear something real and we're halfway through the first set—it was awesome— Art had the cord of his guitar—

PETER: Listen, can we talk later? Moira's going to kill me.

ISABELE: You need to make her understand that we go back.

PETER: I know.

ISABELE: We're all gonna run into each other, small neighborhood. Stay. *(Pulls out a small flask)* Buy ya a drink? It's your favorite liquid breakfast.

PETER: *(Whispering so no one else hears him.)* Bailey's?

ISABELE: It's your second favorite liquid breakfast.

PETER: Coffee?

ISABELE: Whiskey!

PETER: *(Taking the flask from her.)* I'm only staying for a few minutes. *(Drinks)* Thanks.

ISABELE: She all moved in?

PETER: Yeah.

ISABELE: Playing the little lady, home making curtains for her new house?

PETER: Stop it. *(Pause)* You'd like her.

ISABELE: I'm sure I would.

PETER: You look pretty. I like your hair.

ISABELE: I combed it.

PETER: Well, it looks nice.

ISABELE: Imagine if I washed it.

(They smile.)

PETER: So your message last night sounded pretty panicky—and kinda drunk.

ISABELE: We had the show.

PETER: Right. Where again? Lala'z?

ISABELE: Piano's.

PETER: How'd you swing that?

ISABELE: We're good.

PETER: Piano's. Cool.

ISABELE: So I didn't finish. Fire Department comes because apparently the feathered chick collapses at the bar after her set and people are basically *tripping over her* on their way to the back room where we're playing.

PETER: *(Smiling)* Because you're so awesome.

ISABELE: Yeah dick head, because we're so awesome. So we stop playing and are all sitting there having a drink and we get in this *huge fight.*

PETER: About what?

ISABELE: The name of the band.

PETER: Holy Grail?

ISABELE: Catch up, Idol Threat.

PETER: Idle Threat?

ISABELE: I-D-L-E?

PETER: Right.

ISABELE: Right. See, that's the problem. That's how the guys thought it was spelled. It's I-D-O-L. Idol Threat.

PETER: Like Billy Idol?

ISABELE: Like American Idol.

PETER: Maybe you guys should break up.

ISABELE: No. It's *my* band.

PETER: But that's what great bands do—they break up.

ISABELE: We've only been together a couple months.

PETER: Then get back together for the reunion tour.

ISABELE: Bite me. This has to work. We're going to be on top of each other.

PETER: How'd they not know the spelling?

ISABELE: We never had to write it down. They never saw it until they saw the tour schedule. Big meeting about it all tonight.

PETER: Those are always fun.

ISABELE: *(Picking up the book)* Did you read it?

PETER: Kinda.

ISABELE: How do you do that?

PETER: What?

ISABELE: Kinda read a book.

PETER: I skimmed it.

ISABELE: It's *the* book Peter. Instant classic.

PETER: Not really a book person.

ISABELE: The part about the Frisbee. Right on, right?

PETER: What?

ISABELE: The part where they're playing Frisbee on the beach and throw it higher and further than anyone in the history of the world has ever thrown a Frisbee before. It reminds me of us. You didn't even open it. Hello?

PETER: Price is here.

ISABELE: Price?

PETER: Uncle.

(ISABELE *makes noise or physical expression that means* "That's weird.")

PETER: I think it's weird too—why do you think it's weird?

ISABELE: I didn't know you had an uncle.

PETER: Right. It's freaking me out a bit. I mean, I haven't seen this guy *forever.*

ISABELE: What does he want?

PETER: I don't know.

ISABELE: Well, where is he?

PETER: Home, with Moira.

ISABELE: Right. *(Moving closer to him)* I miss you.

PETER: Something's wrong for him to be here.

ISABELE: Are you gonna miss me? Our tour is the fucking shit. Listen to this line up—Athens, Nashville, Chapel Hill, Tampa, Silverlake, Eugene, Olympia, Austin—oh, you should meet us in Austin!

PETER: You know I can't.

ISABELE: Why not? You love Austin.

PETER: I know—

ISABELE: Get your work to send you out, research. They've done it before—

PETER: It's different now.

ISABELE: Now you're married? Jesus. *(Shivering)* It's cold.

PETER: You should wear a coat.

ISABELE: They're too constraining.

PETER: So tell me.

ISABELE: What?

PETER: Why are we here?

ISABELE: Because you said you didn't want to eat so we're just sitting—

PETER: That's not what I mean.

ISABELE: Everyone's been saying this place is—

PETER: Isabele—

ISABELE: What—

PETER: Stop!

ISABELE: Peter—what the fuck is your problem?

PETER: Listen to yourself, you sound crazy.

ISABELE: You...sound crazy...

PETER: *(Overlapping)* You sound crazy—

ISABELE: You sound crazy—

PETER: You sound crazy—

ISABELE: You sound crazy—

(They start laughing.)

ISABELE: Let's sneak into the pool.

PETER: I was there last night.

ISABELE: I haven't been in so long.

PETER: Don't tempt me.

ISABELE: This'll be perfect!

PETER: We'd have to bring food—

ISABELE: Stay for hours. I wonder if that fucked up mural we made is still there—

PETER: It is—

ISABELE: Let's grab some beer, call Nico, Jack—

PETER: Stop, stop, stop. I have like two minutes left in me. I have to go.

ISABELE: You're on a short leash these days.

PETER: Stop.

ISABELE: Fine. I want to ask you something.

PETER: Alright. Out with it.

ISABELE: O K.

PETER: You'll actually have to talk, use words.

ISABELE: Right.

PETER: I don't speak your fairy language.

ISABELE: Ok. You know I'm leaving tomorrow.

PETER: Yes.

ISABELE: Do you remember at Rubela last month— when I was just about to leave and you were smoking a bowl with some Asian chick in that tent?

PETER: Hmmmm. Sounds like it could've happened.

ISABELE: Remember, I had to go 'cause I'd gotten sick?

PETER: Almost...

ISABELE: You don't remember?

PETER: Was this the night that Jack was locked on the roof all night?

ISABELE: Yeah.

PETER: Then I have no recollection.

ISABELE: Oh.

PETER: The last thing I remember was putting on some Sonic Youth C D.

ISABELE: I'd been thinking about what you said— when we were waiting for my car.

PETER: What'd I say?

ISABELE: Nothing.

PETER: Come on—was it funny?

ISABELE: No.

PETER: You know how funny I get.

ISABELE: It was sweet. You expressed your undying love for me. Told me I was the only one in the world that underst—

PETER: *(Laughing)* That's hysterical! I didn't cry or anything, did I?

ISABELE: No, no crying.

PETER: So what about that?

ISABELE: What.

PETER: Why'd you bring it up?

ISABELE: No reason. Nothing. Honest mistake.

PETER: There's something else—

ISABELE: Kinda.

PETER: I'm not telepathic. You're acting like a girl.

ISABELE: Fuck you. Fine. So, I'm leaving tomorrow, gone forever—

PETER: Forever? Really.

ISABELE: Whatever. I just...I want to leave knowing exactly what your feelings for me are.

PETER: Why are you doing this—

ISABELE: I think I have a right—

PETER: God, Isabele.

ISABELE: I want to make sure I understand.

PETER: It's like you enjoy uncomfortable situations.

ISABELE: Fuck you.

PETER: I have to go.

ISABELE: Just like that.

PETER: Just like that.

ISABELE: You're really not going to answer me?

PETER: No.

ISABELE: Vintage Peter. Vintage.

PETER: We've been over this! Have had this conversation before!

ISABELE: That was years ago!

PETER: And *nothing has changed.* Oh wait—except I moved in with my girlfriend.

ISABELE: And *that sounds fun.*

PETER: Why do you do this shit. I don't need it.

ISABELE: Peter—

PETER:—I'm sick of leaving you on corners like this. It's like you glory in being abandoned.

(ISABELE *slaps him hard across the face.)*

ISABELE: You silly fucking ass. *(She exits.)*

Scene IV

(3 P M. HOARD'S *real estate office.* HOARD *is talking on the phone with a possible development partner, cigar hanging out of his mouth. His unseen secretary Kristina is about and he may ad-lib in Polish to her. He is looking over large blue prints of the Pool Development site. His left hand is curled and useless.)*

HOARD: You stopped by Ships Mast huh? Good man Friendly. Born and bred on that very block. He's family. Someone that's makin' a pretty penny off the neighborhood boom.
   Have you seen it yet? The last untouched, wide open space in the neighborhood. An entire city block. Back in the day that pool could hold more that six-thousand

eight-hundred people. It's enormous. When I think
about that much space, and what I could do with it
vertically...

I could easily fit four buildings with ten, maybe
twelve units per floor. Sky's the limit on floors. We're
talking about eight hundred dollars a square foot and
me waving goodbye through the back window of my
Little Red Corvette. That's right—condos.

I'll leave a bit of room for some sort of something that
benefits the neighborhood. It'll be a write off.

The way I'm looking at it,the yuppies'll be over here
in no time. And we'll be following the next artist trail.

I need one solid partner in the venture. A silent
partner if you know what I mean. The locals don't mind
a neighborhood guy makin' a little noise—but you—
you might scare 'em off to be honest. I've takin' the
liberty of havin' some blue prints drawn up, nothing
formal, you know—rough sketches of how I see it.
Sure—you can see them, I'll be at the bar later. Let's say
five o'clock?

Yeah, I made the offer last night at the council
meeting—went face to face with some pathetic petition
from a bunch of pain in the ass artist types. They wanna
do some concert or something. Nothing to worry about.
I laid it out to them—and they were all there—the
Polish Alliance, Friends of Greenpoint, McCarren Park
Conservancy, the Soccer Association, the Bocci ball
guys, goddamn *Alcoholics Anonymous* was there.
I showed 'em how they could use the money to better
more prized aspects of the neighborhood. Build 'em
a new statue or somethin'. Neighborhood loves its
statues. O K, see ya later. *(Laughing. To Kristina in Polish:
"We're going to be rich!")*

Scene V

(4 P M. PETER's *loft.* PRICE *and* MOIRA *are hanging out.*
They are drinking coffee out of what looks like miniature
paint cans.)

MOIRA: It's absurd. Coffee served in mini paint cans.

PRICE: It tastes like paint.

MOIRA: It does not. I kinda like it. Don't tell anyone.

PRICE: Why?

MOIRA: I'd hate to be that— *(She has never said this word*
in her entire life and is trying it out for the very first time.)
—hip.

PRICE: Gkar was interesting.

MOIRA: Did you feel like there were babies just
everywhere?

PRICE: Some.

MOIRA: And that adorable little boy in the Che Guevara
T-shirt!

PRICE: I had at least twenty years on the oldest person
there.

MOIRA: That's everywhere around here. Even I'm
starting to feel old.

PRICE: I find that hard to believe.

MOIRA: I don't really mind. I buy revitalizing face
cream. I watch what I eat. I take *Yoga.* Can I tell you
a secret?

PRICE: Of course.

MOIRA: I think I'm ready, ready to make this big step.
(Pause) I want to buy art.

PRICE: That is serious.

MOIRA: I mean, I want to buy art right now. Something that's angst ridden and already framed.

PRICE: *(His playfulness starting to come out.)* I could whip something up.

MOIRA: Something spectacular and moving.

PRICE: A symbol of your generation.

MOIRA: Yes! Big, huge, gigantic.

(MOIRA grabs a measuring tape and hands one end to PRICE.)

MOIRA: Let's see how big it can be! Help me measure.

(They begin to measure.)

PRICE: By a minority?

MOIRA: What?

PRICE: You should definitely buy minority art.

MOIRA: *(Playing along, enjoying herself.)* Huge minority, framed, angst ridden art.

PRICE: Or perhaps, hmmm, this could be interesting, perhaps that's the red herring.

MOIRA: To go minority?

PRICE: Yes. What you need is something by a white, middle-class, *male artist.*

MOIRA: That has committed some sort of crime—

PRICE: He created the work in jail.

MOIRA: Yes!

PRICE: But he just got out—

MOIRA: And is living off a grant—

PRICE: While he is finishing his most prized and original work to date, something every artist must attempt at least once—

MOIRA: The...

PRICE: The...

MOIRA: Crucifixion?

PRICE: Of course, the crucifixion. A self-portrait of a crucifixion. *(They have finished measuring.)*

MOIRA: So what was that?

PRICE: Six by six.

MOIRA: "Now We Are Six."

PRICE: Milne.

MOIRA: *Wheezles and Sneezles*. It's the first poem I knew.

PRICE: As it should be. They taught you very well in Iowa.

MOIRA: Idaho.

PRICE: Right. Idaho. The West.

MOIRA: The Wild West.

PRICE: Even better. The Wild West.

MOIRA: *(Catching a glimpse of the clock.)* God—it's four o'clock. I have got to get something accomplished today. Do you mind if I leave you for a bit? There's a class that starts in twenty minutes—

PRICE: Not at all. I'll be fine.

MOIRA: Make yourself completely at home.

PRICE: I will.

MOIRA: He'll be back soon.

PRICE: It's been hours.

MOIRA: He does this sometimes, gets distracted, you know?

PRICE: He hasn't been home in ten years, yes, I know.

MOIRA: It's such fun hearing about the three of you.

PRICE: Yes.

MOIRA: I would love to meet Michael someday.

PRICE: What?

MOIRA: To meet him.

PRICE: God. He really hasn't told you anything.

MOIRA: What?

PRICE: Michael's...gone.

MOIRA: Gone...

PRICE: I'm sorry—you should've known, how do you not know—

MOIRA: What happened?

PRICE: Michael had gone up to the lake alone. He was in a very difficult place in a young man's life... Touched by genius, barely twenty. We had become so close.... The last time I saw him he was confused—but that's twenty—what you do, who you are is just starting to make sense.

MOIRA: Price you don't have to—

PRICE: *(He proceeds with growing difficulty.)* He had never learned to swim well. Never liked the water, it frightened him for some reason. Once, he must have been six or seven, I had drawn Michael a bath. He crawled up on my lap and I placed him on my knee as I unbuttoned his shirt and... He smiled at me, insisted I sit with him by the tub. He never let go of my index finger—convinced that something terrible would happen if he did. He was so beautiful—his skin—soft...clinging to me. Some men were doing work at a mill near the lake. They said the water was mirror still, that his head, for the longest time was just above the surface, bobbing, not struggling. A current... something... Then just gone. They never found him. It's been ten years and I'm still waiting for him to come in the room, apologizing for being late. I wouldn't let go. If I saw him one more time, I wouldn't let go.

Scene VI

(5 P M. Ships Mast. FRIENDLY *is behind the bar doing a crossword puzzle.* HOARD *has the blue prints spread out and is looking ready for action.)*

HOARD: So what did this guy look like?

FRIENDLY: Normal. Normal in a suit. Tall. City-like.

HOARD: And he's coming back?

FRIENDLY: Yeah. Said he was going to walk around a bit. Sunglasses. He had sunglasses on.

HOARD: How old was he? Sounded my age.

FRIENDLY: My eyes ain't what they used to be.

HOARD: Never admit that Friendly.

FRIENDLY: What?

HOARD: An ailment.

FRIENDLY: A what?

HOARD: An ailment—look it up. See my hand? I don't complain—I just drink with the other one.

FRIENDLY: Why are you so dressy? Goin' to the prom or somethin'?

HOARD: I just happened to be dressed *nicely.*

FRIENDLY: 'Cause you're hiding somethin'. That's what I think.

HOARD: I didn't know Italians thought.

FRIENDLY: Don't make me call the boys...

HOARD: (Laughing) You shoulda heard me on the phone to this guy. I ended by sayin' some shit about how I want to keep those fuckin' iron grates and turn them into a large public art structure.

FRIENDLY: Had a feeling you had your eye on those—

HOARD: I'll get some artsy fuck in there with a blow torch in one hand and a trust fund in the other to fuck it up. He'll end up payin' me to do it.

FRIENDLY: You know, Peter's pretty sure he's got a shot at—

HOARD: A shot at what? Huh?

FRIENDLY: Easy now.

HOARD: I'd bury him before the first guitar passed through the arch.

FRIENDLY: You know what I was thinkin' today? The good 'ole days at the pool... was thinkin' about how warm the concrete would be on your feet.

HOARD: (Laughing) Hot! It could be hot as hell— like walking on coals.

FRIENDLY: Another excuse to stay in the water.

(ISABELE *enters carrying a huge bag loaded with stuff. She sets it on the bar and starts digging through it.*)

FRIENDLY: Isabele! How ya doing?

ISABELE: I'd be a lot better if I could find my goddamn map.

FRIENDLY: Did ya lose your way or somethin'?

ISABELE: (*Pulling clothes and magazines out of her bag*) I'm going on the road, wanna map it out.

FRIENDLY: I know a lot about maps.

HOARD: Jesus Christ.

FRIENDLY: Mapping. I had this uncle—

HOARD: You and your fuckin' Uncle.

FRIENDLY: What about him?

ISABELE: Buddy, he was talking to me. (*To* FRIENDLY) What about him?

FRIENDLY: Uncle Doc—this used to be his bar. Went crazy comin' up with this "map mind," or "mappin' of the mind"—somethin' like that. Drink?

ISABELE: Definitely. Make me a Pixie Stick.

FRIENDLY: A what?

ISABELE: A little vodka, a little soda, a splash of Chambord.

FRIENDLY: (*Starts making her drink*) Fancy.

ISABELE: And throw an olive in it—I'm hungry.

HOARD: It's on me.

ISABELE: Uh, no thanks, I got it. (*Whispering*) Friendly, tab.

HOARD: (*Sneering*) I wanna hear about the map— let's all drink to it.

FRIENDLY: Never touch the stuff when I'm on this side. Uncle Doc had come over in '38—bought a little house for five thousand on Conselyea. Once he settled, he wanted to map his past so we wouldn't forget—like ah what's that thing called that shows all your family—

HOARD: A tree. A family tree.

FRIENDLY: Tree, right. The map was of Italy but he had covered it with little sentences, pictures, wild stories of sneakin' off and living for days on berries and bark. Took up an entire room.

HOARD: Sounds like that crazy guy's office in that shit movie about the beautiful mind.

FRIENDLY: He'd make Tommy and me stare at this wall. It's like 150 fuckin' degrees outside—all we want to do is play ball—we'd just lost the Dodgers—and we're starin' at a wall. Inside—no air conditionin'. So Uncle Doc starts talkin'—tellin' us about his sacrifice. How he'd left Italy to make a better way for his family—and our family's family. All of a sudden he's *cryin'*. He'd wrote down all the names of the people he'd left behind when he came here—all sentimental like. I'll always remember Fontamara. By Fontamara there was this big X.

ISABELE: It's where he left his heart.

HOARD: It's where he left his wallet.

FRIENDLY: It's where he left his first wife. She wouldn't come with him, no joke. Wouldn't leave her family.

ISABELE: And he was heartbroken.

FRIENDLY: Never think he did recover. He'd made this sacrifice. *For us.*

HOARD: World's full of sacrifice. Good piece of property this here bar.

(NICO *enters.*)

ISABELE: Nico! My favorite orphan.

FRIENDLY: Hey there.

NICO: Hey guys. Isabele—tomorrow right, you leave tomorrow?

ISABELE: Yep, sit, drink.

NICO: Tempting. I can't quite hit it yet.

ISABELE: Come on. Toast my farewell. It's only fair.

NICO: Later, I promise. Have you seen Peter?

ISABELE: *(Raising her glass)* I'm fairly sure I drank him. He's tiny and green with a pimento inside, right?

NICO: I want to go see Jolly Roger with him.

ISABELE: Fuck him and everyone else's band.

NICO: Isabele, Idle Threat's great—

ISABELE: You haven't even *seen* us.

NICO: Well, it's a good *name* for a band.

ISABELE: Whatever. *(Brightening a bit)* Has he told you about Moira yet?

NICO: That she moved in?

ISABELE: O-V-E-R. Done. No longer.

NICO: What do ya mean?

ISABELE: Strict word that we're not to talk to her. You even look at her. It's off. She's dead.

NICO: Dead.

ISABELE: You know what I mean.

NICO: Dead to Peter.

HOARD: Friendly, another.

NICO: I don't get it.

ISABELE: We can't get everything Nico, you know Peter.

NICO: I should find him.

ISABELE: Fine. Go. I'll drop ya a postcard.

(NICO heads for the door.)

ISABELE: Don't forget about Moira.

NICO: I won't.

ISABELE: I'm just telling ya what he said.

NICO: I know. *(He exits.)*

ISABELE: *(Very pleased with herself)* Friendly, the rest of the story please. Did he ever marry again?

FRIENDLY: Uncle Doc's second wife, he met her here, spoke not *one word* of English. Still can't. She makes fresh Mozzarella, sells it out of some dirty storefront ever since Doc died.

ISABELE: That's sad.

HOARD: That's life. My drink?

FRIENDLY: I think about that sometimes—what he's done for us. How he'd just look at that wall, his map, and cry. *(Clears his throat)*

HOARD: *(With growing impatience)* Where the hell is that guy.

FRIENDLY: We stopped goin' over after awhile. Couldn't take it anymore. Too hard for some reason. Maybe it was just too damn hot.

Scene VII

(6 P M. Blow Yoga Studio. MOIRA *has just entered a class in progress and is quietly unrolling her mat.)*

V O: *(Voice Over of the yoga instructor.)* Now that the spine's relaxed let us move out of of Supta Badha Konasana. Guide your body up to Sukhasana, before we transition into Balasana. We're opening the pelvis. Feel it. Make sure your "sit" bones are well grounded. Give each butt cheek a little tug, assuring you are in the correct position.

Close your eyes travel back to your own warm womb

of birth, to the beginning of your personal journey,
transforming you into the vessel you are today.
I see some new faces in class today. Breath...
Now let's slide into Balasana.
    I'm Janaki, Jenny to some, so happy to have you here.
I see you are all in different stages of incubation. You
glow—each of you. I just want to take a moment to
welcome all you young mothers.

(MOIRA *raises her head, alarmed.*)

V O: I'm sure you are feeling full and fulfilled.
Gently pull up and move into Cat/Cow.
    After class, be sure to stop by the front desk to
purchase the latest "must-have yogacessory" —Prenatal
Yoga Cards. They're compact, concise and full of tips
for baby and you.
    You'll find this class is not only a way to build a
foundation that will support you during the difficult
and *extremely painful* time of delivery, but will also
introduce you to other expecting mothers creating a
community that empowers you through the journey
that is your pregnancy.

(MOIRA *becomes increasingly taken in by the instructor and
hardly removes her hand from her abdomen.*)

V O: Breathe... Let your mind expand, allow the breath
to travel through your center, bless your creation.
Follow it to a place of serenity. Your secret place of
happiness, calm. Encourage your mind to guide you
back to where you're from and what makes you—you.
And bring your baby with you...

Scene VIII

(7 P M. PETER'*s hanging out on the street listening to his headphones.* NICO *enters and taps him on the shoulder, he jumps.)*

PETER: Holy shit. *Don't* fucking do that man.

NICO: Sorry—

PETER: Dude—I just saw 'em. Ran fucking into them on the street.

NICO: Jolly Roger?

PETER: I went to their studio. It's a dump. *It's* on. They're on.

NICO: Nice. What's their sound?

PETER: It's not only sound—it's *all* of it. First of all— they just moved here—I *know* they're from Connecticut.

NICO: You're from Connecticut—

*(*PETER *whacks him playfully on the side of the head.)*

PETER: Whatever. Just picture it—shaggy hair, prep school, designer grunge mother fuckers. Everyone *loves* them. You'd think these guys were the goddamn *Beatles. Shit.*

NICO: How many of 'em?

PETER: Four.

NICO: Perfect. They sound great.

PETER: The best part? *They just stand there on stage.*

NICO: Motionless?

PETER: Stationary.

NICO: You're due man—

PETER: It only takes one. One big sign and I'm golden.

NICO: Ya think this's it?

PETER: Yep. And underneath their stylized monotone, guess.

NICO: Tell me!

PETER: Sirens. Mermaids—sounds like fucking virgins purring on a rock.

NICO: Like that movie.

PETER: Which one?

NICO: The, ah, the one with George Clooney on that odyssey. You know, they see the chicks and John Turturro like melts into the water or something with them.

PETER: Dude—you've been working at the video store too long—

NICO: A lot of people started in video stores. Tarantino.

PETER: Tarantino's sucks. Nico—everyone fucking loves these guys. *Crap.* Their moms come to the shows, looking all funny at their goddamn bandmates, masturbating under the table.

NICO: Sounds like you couldn't cast 'em better.

PETER: I mean—their approach is *all wrong.* They're trying too hard—

NICO: You can authenticize them.

PETER: Damn straight.

NICO: When are you seeing 'em next?

PETER: Drinks on Tuesday. Fucking shoe-gazers. They're perfect for Region.

NICO: I'm off Tuesday.

PETER: We'll see.

NICO: Dude, come on.

PETER: Alright—

(His phone rings. He glances at it.)

PETER: I have to take this—let's catch up later—

NICO: Hey, I heard about Moir—

PETER: *(Turning away to answer the phone.)* Yo.

(NICO hesitates then exits. Lights up on MOIRA who is crouched in the bathroom stall at Blow Yoga. She is on her cell and has just taken a pregnancy test. The remnants of the box scattered around her.)

MOIRA: Peter?

PETER: Hey!

MOIRA: *(Smiling)* I have to tell you something.

PETER: *(Having trouble hearing her)* Moira? Hello?

MOIRA: Can you hear me?

PETER: There you are.

MOIRA: I think I might be pregnant.

PETER: Who is this?

MOIRA: Peter, it's me.

PETER: Pregnant?

MOIRA: *(With increasing excitement)* I'm kinda scared, where are you? I just took it and I feel kinda funny, like what if this is some sign and we're supposed to change our lives right now and start looking after something else, something small, ours. This could be the change—

PETER: Your cutting in and out—

MOIRA: A change, a turning point—

PETER: A what—

MOIRA: *Turning point—*

PETER: You mean those guys that played last night—

MOIRA: No, it's not the name of a band. I just took it, so just like two more minutes.

(The rest of the dialogue is overlapping.)

PETER: Moira? *(Holds cell phone up looking for service.)* Moira?

MOIRA: Peter? Peter, are you there? Peter?

(PETER sighs and flips his cell phone closed.)

Scene IX

(7:30 P M. PETER's loft. PRICE is sitting alone drinking Jack Daniels. He has polished off most of the bottle. PETER enters.)

PETER: Yo—took a little longer, sorry.

PRICE: It's been seven hours.

PETER: I said I'm sorry man.

PRICE: I brought you something.

(Sets a bag of marbles on the table. PETER picks them up.)

PETER: Where'd you get these?

PRICE: Drink? I think it's time we had a drink together.

PETER: I thought...I threw them in the lake.

PRICE: They drained it last week, they're developing the area.

PETER: I'll have a drink. *(He pours a glass. He dumps out the bag of marbles and examines them.)* Yep—these are his.

PRICE: Michael's?

PETER: Who else's?

PRICE: You still can't say his name.

PETER: Jesus Christ.

PRICE: You want to play?

PETER: You want to play with me? You sure I'm good enough? Did some shrink tell you you should come down here and play marbles with me?

PRICE: No shrink. I thought it might be nice.

PETER: The game's back ya know.

PRICE: Back?

PETER: Back. Marbles, Jacks, Paddle Ball. "Batteries Not Included, Retro Game Night, Tuesdays at Larry's." I haven't played though, it's been years.

PRICE: Forever.

(They both take huge drinks.)

PETER: I always liked Conqueror—

PRICE: That's a good one.

PETER: And Spanners. Spanners rocked.

PRICE: Bounce About—

PETER: Hundreds—

PRICE: One Step—

PETER: Dobblers—

PRICE: Odds or Evens—

PETER: Pyramid—

PRICE: Spanners.

PETER: I said that.

PRICE: You did?

PETER: Bounce About.

PRICE: I said that. I'm glad I found them.

PETER: Me too.

PRICE: It's been too long.

PETER: Let's play Conqueror.

PRICE: Pick your taw.

PETER: Age before beauty, you pick.

(PRICE *selects his shooting marble.*)

PETER: See this one? I still have a bump from where that asshole hit me on the head with it.

PRICE: We'll just divide them in half.

PETER: You go first.

PRICE: I had the pick, you take the first shot.

PETER: Remind me.

PRICE: How to play?

PETER: Yeah.

PRICE: You roll the marble out, any distance you want, but remember you have to hit it with the taw—

PETER: Right. And if I hit it, it's mine.

PRICE: And if you don't it stays in the field.

PETER: Then you roll one out and go for it—

PRICE: Exactly. Once a marble is hit you get to keep it, or them, depending on if you hit more than one.

PETER: And we play to the death.

PRICE: To the death.

(PETER *jumps up and puts music on.*)

PRICE: It seems I've drank a majority of the bottle during my wait for you.

PETER: We have some gin. Moira's a gin girl.

PRICE: She struck me as a vodka girl.

PETER: Should be, she's from Idaho. Fuckin' potatoes. She's a good girl.

PRICE: A keeper. I hate gin.

PETER: So do I.

(They finish off the rest of the Jack.)

PETER: I'll get it.

PRICE: You realize what tomorrow is.

(PETER is retrieving the gin and pouring it.)

PETER: I've been waiting for that. Thought we'd throw one back and cheer ole Michael. See how I said that? *Michael.* Are we having a birthday party? Mom bakin' a cake?

PRICE: No.

PETER: What then?

PRICE: Night before last I had a dream. It's the day after Michael died. I'm home and the doorbell rings. I answer it and standing in front of me is Michael... white and puffy from all the water. He's wearing that old green Springsteen shirt.

PETER: I loved that shirt.

PRICE: I freeze, just stare at him. He walks in laughing and talking about how he'd just been swimming and how he didn't know why he'd been such a baby about water all these years and how *he'd just loved it.* "Had a blast Price, an adventure." He walks into the living room, sits down on the carpet and pulls out his bag of marbles.
   We start playing... Then I realize...*he does not know that he has died.* And I can't tell him. He stays for a year.

PETER: Your dream lasted a year?

PRICE: We don't leave the house once. And no one comes to look for us. As the date that Michael drowned starts coming up again, he begins to act strange. More sullen and withdrawn. Like he knows what's coming and that it's going to happen again. I don't know what to do. The night before the anniversary of his drowning Michael sits silent. I can't get him to speak. He lays beside me, holding on to just my index finger—doesn't let go. Just before dawn he gets up and walks to the front door. I follow him. He leaves the house and walks down to the lake. I somehow know, in the dream, that I can't do anything, that I can't stop him. And he walks into the water. He walks in so peacefully, the water is so calm. And then...he's gone, and I wake up.

PETER: Price I don't know why you're here but I think it's creepy—

PRICE: Come on Michael!

PETER: *What?!*

PRICE: Peter—

PETER: Did you really just call me *Michael*?

PRICE: No—

PETER: She used to do that—

PRICE: I was saying that Michael—

PETER: The entire summer after.

(They are quiet for a moment.)

PRICE: It's hard to believe you haven't been back, not once.

PETER: *(Drinks)* Not too hard.

PRICE: Why?

PETER: What am I going to do in Connecticut? Start a *family*? Buy a house? Become a scholar like you? Fish?

This, right here, is where I belong. My community.
What a horrible word, *community*.

PRICE: You don't miss her?

PETER: Look, I tried to go back once. This notion had
come to me—I want to say in a dream, but I think I
might have been awake. I'd go back at night—sneak
through the open window to my room, then curl up
in bed as though I'd never left. She'd find me in the
morning and she'd let out a cry that would break your
fuckin' heart. Her famous boy had returned—and she'd
look ten years younger and happy—maybe more
proud—she'd throw on her best dress and insist on
taking me all around, show me off. I even got my hair
cut at Jinny's the night before—she cuts Lunar Eclipse's
hair. All spiked and messy and important. (*Grabs the
bottle, taking a huge swig.*) And I was almost at the door,
knob in hand, chain off, and the truth just...hit.
Pummeled really. I wasn't *anything.* (*This is the weakest
we ever see* PETER.) I was thinking how it was all *just*
about to change. How I was like this early Quincy
Jones—before Michael Jackson—and would be worth
millions one day. But, for now, I was just *Peter.* And
she'd probably be pissed I hadn't called. Pissed I hadn't
become a doctor or whatever the fuck Michael had
wanted to be. So, I threw down my bag and went to
meet Isabele for a drink at Ship's Mast. Friendly was
working and that seemed about as close to home as
I was going to get. People know me here.

PRICE: Here—in New York?

PETER: Here. In the neighborhood. They see me and
they want to talk to me. They know that *I know.*

PRICE: Know what?

PETER: Answers Price. Answers that they'll never have.

PRICE: You've lost me here.

PETER: It's like this—a couple years ago I was wearing this hat. Big, foamy trucker-esque looking John Deere hat. Found it on the street. It was dirty and smelly *and hot.*

PRICE: You're wearing a smelly hat.

PETER: I wear this hat all day, out that night—everywhere. The next day I'm walking to the subway and I see like ten people wearing that same goddamn hat. The next couple years the hat is *everywhere*—San Francisco, Detroit, Seattle. People stop wearing it here because they now think that the hat is *passé.* I keep wearing the hat.

PRICE: The smelly hat.

PETER: I wear the hat 'cause I like the goddamn hat. And—who'd of guessed it—wham!—the hat's back.

PRICE: Help me here.

PETER: The hat never really went anywhere. *I knew that.* People got scared—that the hat had run it's course. Have you seen the cover of *Time Out*?

PRICE: No.

PETER: It's on it.

PRICE: What?

PETER: The hat's on the fucking cover. Just sitting there, smoking. *(Starts laughing)* The hat's smoking a cigarette.

PRICE: *(Drinks)* She asked me to come see you.

PETER: My mom?

PRICE: It's Michael.

PETER: What?

PRICE: When they drained the lake—

PETER: Holy shit.

PRICE: Your mother's having a service.

PETER: Of course she is.

PRICE: I want you to come back with me.

PETER: There must have been nothing left of him.

PRICE: They matched dental records.

PETER: And you want me to go to Michael's funeral.
Again.

PRICE: Memorial. It would mean a lot.

PETER: *(Begins putting the marbles back in the bag)* O K.
O K, O K, O K, O K. I need to, ah, go to the bar.

PRICE: The bar?

PETER: Yeah. I need to be there. *(Drinking from the bottle)*

PRICE: Alright.

PETER: I need a drink.

PRICE: O K.

PETER: O K.

(PETER shoves the marbles in his pocket and they exit.)

Scene X

*(8 P M. The bench in the park near Exxon Cafe. MOIRA's
sitting, still in her pajamas/yoga clothes, looking a bit
disheveled. NICO enters.)*

MOIRA: Nico?

(NICO is unsure of what to do and freezes.)

MOIRA: Nico? *(He attempts to hide.)*

MOIRA: Nico, I can see you. What are you doing?

NICO: *(Whispering)* Shhhh. Is anyone around?

MOIRA: What?

NICO: I'm not supposed to talk to you.

MOIRA: Why? Is this some sort of game?

NICO: You know why.

MOIRA: Nico. Come here, sit with me. *(No answer)*
I think I'm going crazy.

NICO: I heard.

MOIRA: You what?

NICO: Small neighborhood.

MOIRA: Nico, come out here.

NICO: I just want to make sure you're alright.

MOIRA: What are you talking about?

NICO: Isabele told me.

MOIRA: Told you what exactly.

NICO: *Peter*, that it didn't work out, *you know—*

MOIRA: That is absolutely *not* true, I just moved in!

NICO: *(Coming out of hiding)* Damnit. Every fucking time.

MOIRA: Why do you listen to her. She speaks nonsense.
We're great. We're fine. I don't know. I'm confused.

NICO: I totally understand.

MOIRA: Understand what?

NICO: I don't know. I'm confused too. I'm trying to
channel it, the confusion. Use it, ya know, put it in
my treatment. I'm working on a film idea—

MOIRA: That's great—

NICO: It's about this kid. He's young, approaching
thirty and convinced that nothing's ever happened
to him in his entire life.

MOIRA: Nothing?

NICO: You know, he's always in the bathroom when that great, unforgettable home run is hit. Like he didn't even know that the Domino Sugar Factory shut down 'til it hit the market for millions and bands like Fischer Spooner, Wit, and D J Larry Tee—he didn't even know them until Luxx had closed and become Trash. Big things constantly happen when he's just around the corner.

MOIRA: He's on the verge of something then.

NICO: Maybe.

MOIRA: *Something* has to happen to him if nothing ever has.

NICO: But when?

MOIRA: It's your movie.

NICO: It is. It's just an idea.

MOIRA: I like it. That's the fun of it, finding out what happens to him.

NICO: Yeah... Have you been sitting here long?

MOIRA: A while, I guess. The park's kinda gross, but the bench is nice. I think I'm... *(She smiles.)* A little homesick.

NICO: That's it! Maybe this guy's homesick too.

MOIRA: Are you?

NICO: I don't know...I don't know what that means really.

MOIRA: You'd like the West.

NICO: I like it when you talk about it.

MOIRA: It's the biggest sky there is. So much space. There are certain places you stumble on where I swear to god no one has ever been. Like you're the first one there. Ever.

NICO: Really?

MOIRA: And the mountains are enormous, these majestic ranges with names like *Sawtooth* and *Blackfoot*.

NICO: And people climb them?

MOIRA: Of course.

NICO: Maybe this guy, in the movie, would like to do that.

(They are quiet for a moment. He pulls a piece of paper out of his back pocket.)

NICO: Check this out.

MOIRA: "For the protection of our village from the plague of the artists." What is this?

NICO: The Hasids are posting it all over the Southside. It basically says were ruining their lives—

MOIRA: *(Reading)* "...have mercy upon us and upon the borders of our village and do not allow the persecution to come inside our home—please remove from upon us the plague of the artists." Wow.

NICO: I know, right?

MOIRA: "So that we shall not drown in evil waters—and so that they shall not come to our residence to ruin it." God.

NICO: It's hanging over the register at the video store next to a Harvey Pekar cartoon.

MOIRA: It's intense.

NICO: I think I'll put it in my movie.

MOIRA: *(Handing it back to him)* Cool.

NICO: Buy you a drink? Might dull the confusion.

MOIRA: God, I'm still a little jittery from last night.

NICO: That's it! You have "The Fear".

MOIRA: "The Fear?"

NICO: In Ireland they call it "The Bleedin' Terrors." Do you feel like everyone's looking at you?

MOIRA: Kinda—

NICO: Like everything you've ever done in your *entire life* has been a mistake?

MOIRA: Not *everything*—

NICO: Peter says you can smell "The Fear." (*Smells her*) I think you have it—

MOIRA: What do I do?!

NICO: You need a drink. Only thing that fixes it. (*Standing and offering his arm*) May I escort you, my lady?

MOIRA: In a minute, can we just sit here for a sec?

NICO: Sure. (*The thought of sitting still for a minute had never occurred to him before.*) Tell me about the West. About all that space.

Scene XI

(*10 P M. Ship's Mast.* ISABELE *is smashed and* HOARD *is growing meaner.* HOARD *has the blueprints of the Condo complex on the bar and a deck of cards. At this point,* ISABELE's *map has become a very large drink coaster.*)

FRIENDLY: This round's on me, again. Same?

ISABELE: Why not. Hoard, you're missing the point entirely, everyone hates you because of this—

HOARD: I'm the only one taking this neighborhood seriously. To the next level.

ISABELE: It's perfect as is.

HOARD: You've been here all of five minutes.

ISABELE: Eight years.

(HOARD *grunts.*)

ISABELE: Condos?

HOARD: Yep.

ISABELE: You're high, that's like bringing in a Starbucks.

HOARD: Done deal.

FRIENDLY: Not quite. I got some connections, an inside track, they're giving us a call tonight. 'Member when they were tryin' to have that M-T-V show around here?

ISABELE: The Real World—

HOARD: That's what I'm talking about, *this is the real world.* Fucking kids coming in—

ISABELE: I've lived here forever.

HOARD: Eight years is not forever.

ISABELE: I basically discovered it.

HOARD: Jesus. I was born here.

FRIENDLY: *This* is the way it goes. The way it's always been. People are here, then new people come, then people *leave.* It's a— (*Looking for the word*) It's a—

HOARD: A cycle. It's a fucking cycle. (*Raising his glass*) Might as well make some money off it.

FRIENDLY: Might as well.

HOARD: Just wait, this bar'll be a tourist destination.

(NICO *and* MOIRA *enter.*)

NICO: Whatever my lady wants Friendly. She's got "The Fear," take it away.

FRIENDLY: With pleasure.

MOIRA: A gin and tonic please.

NICO: Beer me.

FRIENDLY: Comin' up.

ISABELE: Containment. The new attitude needs to be one of containment. We can't keep encouraging these newbies to think they can just move here.

NICO: (To MOIRA) I wanna show you something.

FRIENDLY: Ya can't keep adding plants to the garden.

MOIRA: What is it?

NICO: (Pulling some papers out of his back pocket) Check this out. It's my treatment.

MOIRA: Very exciting.

ISABELE: Do you remember that movie where all those people lived in a bubble under water?

HOARD: Don't watch movies. I work.

ISABELE: The boat, or whatever, had capsized—but it sank in such a way that most of the ship remained untouched by water.

MOIRA: This is amazing.

NICO: You think so?

ISABELE: Landed upside down I think and made this bubble people could live in—

HOARD: What goddamn bubble?

ISABELE: —Hundreds of people live there, had a whole system for everything.

(MOIRA sneezes.)

FRIENDLY: Salute.

ISABELE: And every time someone had the slightest symptom of sickness— *(Mimes slicing of her throat)* —they just kill 'em.

HOARD: Ahh-huh! Kill her.

NICO: Isabele—you make that story up too?

ISABELE: No, it's *that movie*. It might have been a T V movie.

NICO: Yeah. A T V movie. Sounds right for you.

ISABELE: *(Ignoring NICO, acknowledging MOIRA)* Hey.

MOIRA: Hi.

HOARD: Hi.

MOIRA: Hey.

ISABELE: *(To MOIRA)* Ah, little tip for the new pad: watch the third step from the top when your going up the stairs, it's a bit higher than rest, wouldn't want you to trip.

MOIRA: Sorry to hear you're leaving, tomorrow right?

ISABELE: Yep.

FRIENDLY: She's got it all mapped out.

MOIRA: Get your book?

ISABELE: I did. I sure did. Thanks for letting him out of the house. Friendly, can I get the darts? Feel like hitting something.

FRIENDLY: You should come upstate with me sometime, go hunting. It's satisfying.

ISABELE: Tempting. *(Sauntering over to the dart board)*

HOARD: So when's the call coming in?

FRIENDLY: Should be very soon.

NICO: What call?

FRIENDLY: About the pool.

NICO: I thought they wouldn't know 'til Monday.

FRIENDLY: I got a cousin that's friends with the aunt of that scrawny little councilman with the circle glasses and the huge nose—

HOARD: *(Starts shuffling his deck of cards)* Szaro.

FRIENDLY: Right. Szaro.

HOARD: I fucked Szaro's sister in that pool.

MOIRA: Nico, maybe a drink isn't the best idea—

NICO: No, no, no—take a sip—

HOARD: In the deep end.

NICO: I promise it helps, like medicine.

MOIRA: My medicine.

(She drinks. PETER and PRICE enter. They are extremely drunk. HOARD deals himself a hand of Solitaire.)

FRIENDLY: There he is!

PETER: Yo!

FRIENDLY: On cue, Hoard's been moving in on the beautiful ladies at the bar—

NICO: Yo!

PETER: *(Seeing ISABELE first)* What are you doing here?

MOIRA: Peter!

PETER: There you are!

MOIRA: Where have you been? Why haven't you called me back?

PETER: Price poured a bottle of gin down my throat.

ISABELE: You hate gin.

PETER: Blame him.

PRICE: I did not.

MOIRA: Perfect.

HOARD: Jesus fucking Christ, it's goddamn Family Fued.

MOIRA: It's been hours.

PETER: Have I got a story. Price does *not* disappoint.

PRICE: Peter.

MOIRA: You're drunk.

PETER: Pretty much.

ISABELE: I love it! I still haven't been to bed, have you?

PETER: Shit no -

MOIRA: What do you mean?

ISABELE: Get 'em all a round—on Hoard.

HOARD: Just the ladies. That includes Peter.

PETER: And we're off!

FRIENDLY: The usual?

PETER: Why not. Ok, I'm going to give you all three guesses what Price's story is.

FRIENDLY: *(To* PRICE*)* And you?

ISABELE: Give us a clue.

PRICE: Water. Peter. Stop.

PETER: No clues.

ISABELE: *(Slurring)* Have a drink Price. You're Price, I've never had a drink with a Price.

PETER: Have one.

PRICE: A Scotch, neat.

FRIENDLY: Comin' up.

PETER: Give him a double.

MOIRA: I'm missing something here.... You go missing, Nico thinks we broke up—

PETER: What?

NICO: I—

ISABELE: *What* Nico?

NICO: She told me that. Said Moira was dead. To you.

(ISABELE *quietly laughs, amused.*)

PETER: What?

NICO: She said you guys broke up—

PETER: Isabele. Really.

ISABELE: Let me guess: Price is here to give you millions of dollars of inheritance from a distant rel—

PETER: Close, but not close. Two guesses left. *(Holding up the bag of marbles)* Whoever gets it wins a shiny bag of marbles.

PRICE: Don't do this.

MOIRA: *(To* NICO*)* This day...is so...

NICO: I know...

MOIRA: Peter?

PETER: What did I do now? *(Picking her up and spinning her around.)*

MOIRA: Put me down—

PETER: How was Yoga?

MOIRA: Our conversation? We got cut off?

ISABELE: That's what he does when he doesn't want to talk to you anymore.

PETER: Shut up.

MOIRA: Stay out of this!

PETER: What are you talking about?

(ISABELE *makes a face at him, he starts laughing.*)

PETER: Now you—you are drunk.

ISABELE: Minced, wrecked, legless. I just started...drinking.

PETER: You can't say your J's when your drunk—

MOIRA: What's going on?

ISABELE: *(Like her tongue is too big for her mouth.)* Just.

NICO: He's drunk, it's O K....

MOIRA: Peter, we got cut off?

ISABELE: Just.

MOIRA: Aren't you even curious?

ISABELE: Jack-o'-lantern.

PETER: Fucking tour.

ISABELE: Jesus.

PETER: You're not going anywhere, you're a drunken pixie.

ISABELE: Not a pixie— *(Raising her glass)* A Pixie Stick.

PETER: *(Seeing* HOARD*)* Hoard! You old bastard.

HOARD: Excuse me?

PETER: *(Walking over and seeing the blueprints.)* That's a lot of work for nothing man.

HOARD: Did you just call me a bastard?

FRIENDLY: Easy now—

HOARD: You fuckin' punk.

PETER: What?

PRICE: Alright, we should go.

MOIRA: Peter, can I talk to you outside?

PETER: I just came from outside.

MOIRA: Why are you doi—

HOARD: *(Rising from his stool)* Don't you *ever* call me a bastard—

PETER: Polock.

ISABELE: *(She starts laughing hysterically.)* You're killing me, stop!

(The phone at the bar rings, everyone looks at it.)

PETER: What?

FRIENDLY: *(To PETER)* The board's decision's coming in.

PETER: Fucking board.

HOARD: Get it!

FRIENDLY: *(Picking up the phone)* Ships Mast. Uh-huh. *(To everyone at the bar)* Not them. *(Into phone)* No, we don't have Galaga.

HOARD: Jesus Christ.

PETER: The board don't mean shit.

HOARD: You hipster fuck.

PETER: You're a little late with the word "hipster"—

ISABELE: So last year.

PETER: The correct term is... *(He says a word but it is muffled and not heard.)*

FRIENDLY: Peter, have some respect—

PETER: Respect? Fuck that.

HOARD: Watch yourself in my bar.

FRIENDLY: It's actually my bar.

MOIRA: Peter, can we go, now?

HOARD: You bring your filthy hair and your girl-scout shirts into the neighborhood. Bunch of little faggots you are.

FRIENDLY: Hoard.

ISABELE: He's definitely *not* a fag.

MOIRA: Peter—

PETER: Say it again Hoard.

FRIENDLY: Hoard, stop it.

HOARD: Shut up.

PETER: What? Whatcha got?

PRICE: Drop it Peter. We can still catch the midnight train.

MOIRA: Train?

PRICE: Home.

ISABELE: Ooh, ooh—second guess: Strange Uncle Price has arrived in vain attempt to bring wayward nephew home for new life. Did I win?

PRICE: Peter has to come home.

PETER: Fuck that.

MOIRA: What are you talking about?

PRICE: There is a memorial tomor—

MOIRA: Home?

ISABELE: *(This is the funniest thing she has ever heard in her entire life.)* You are not going home.

MOIRA: Nico, does "The Fear" make everyone seem crazy?

PETER: I'm not going anywhere.

MOIRA: Does it make you want to cry?

NICO: It can make you feel small.

ISABELE: Price! You are Priceless!

PETER: *(Downing his whisky)* Fill me up.

MOIRA: Let's go home.

ISABELE: This is home, we are home.

PETER: *(Toasting her)* Well said.

(NICO is removing the empty glasses off ISABELE's map, engrossed by it.)

MOIRA: DID YOU FORGET???

PETER: What?

MOIRA: The test.

PETER: Fuck.

(ISABELE rests her head on the bar.)

MOIRA: The pregnancy test.

PETER: The test.

PRICE: What?

(HOARD starts to laugh a low, evil chuckle.)

NICO: *(Engrossed in the map)* Idaho! I found it.

ISABELE: This could be a song... *(Starts humming and passes out)*

MOIRA: We get cut off when I have two minutes left to wait and I see you hours later?

PETER: What happened?

PRICE: You're—

PETER: Drinking! You're drinking—I see a drink in your hand! Thank god! *(Dances around)*

MOIRA: Thank God?

(HOARD *laughs a little louder.*)

PETER: Thank God. *(To* HOARD*)* Shut up!

PRICE: Are you alright?

PETER: Of course she's alright. Come here—

(Opens his arms to MOIRA. *She does not go.)*

PETER: —I'm so glad.

MOIRA: Glad?

PETER: Relieved, overwhelmed, happy, exuberant. Let's have champagne!

MOIRA: Peter, this could all be so exciting. You, me, we're building this future... Something great is happening, I can feel it.

(Uncomfortable silence.)

FRIENDLY: They're messy, Moira love, babies—

PETER: Jesus Moria.

MOIRA: Champagne?

PETER: You didn't actually want it? I don't even have *plants*—there's a reason for that.

NICO: *(Oblivious and absorbed in the map)* So much space. So far away, Peter, it's this far away. *(Indicating with his hands)*

HOARD: You're other girlfriend's gone over here.

PETER: *(Noticing* ISABELE *is passed out, he claps his hands near her ear a few times in an attempt to wake her. She moans.)* Great.

MOIRA: There's so much room at the loft, it would—

PETER: Are you kidding? Have we met? Moira, I want adventure— *(Gulps half his whiskey)* —I'm gonna break this place open. I go to shows and drink in this bar and wake up in the pool with the sun coming over the wall.

And at the end of the day you are there and you're so sweet and warm...and...and Jolly Roger's gonna change my life. Right Nico?

NICO: *(Not listening)* Right. Um, what?

MOIRA: And I'm not.

HOARD: No one's waking up in that pool until I put condos over it.

PETER: Not what?

MOIRA: Going to change your life.

PETER: You're my...you're my...

MOIRA: What. What am I to you?

(ISABELE raises her head from the bar.)

ISABELE: You're his fucking mother.

PETER: Fuck you.

PRICE: Peter, we should go.

NICO: We should go West!

MOIRA: Go WHERE?

PETER: I'm not going anywhere. Why does everyone want to take me somewhere?

PRICE: *(Touching PETER's shoulder)* Peter—

PETER: Don't touch me. No one touch me.

HOARD: I think you should all go. This isn't your home. This is mine. I deserve more— *(Hiccups)* Respect.

FRIENDLY: You'd be working for the M T A if these kids hadn't moved here.

HOARD: Well they did. And I've got some idiot fuck down on Kent paying two Gs a month to live in a musty topless bar. Who's the idiot. Don't tell me—

FRIENDLY: Hoard.

HOARD: What? You fucking Snowbird. His bar tab bought you your condo.

FRIENDLY: Get out.

HOARD: *(To* PETER*)* Yeah, get out.

FRIENDLY: Hoard. Get out.

*(*PETER *starts laughing.)*

HOARD: Excuse me?

FRIENDLY: I can't have this.

HOARD: Have what?

FRIENDLY: This! This situation. Can't go back to how it was, two customers every night.

HOARD: I was raised in this bar—

PETER: Raised pretty much everywhere, weren't ya. The pool, this bar—

FRIENDLY: Peter!

PETER: You heard him. Get the fuck out.

HOARD: This is a joke—

FRIENDLY: *(Struggling)* I have my responsibilities here.

PETER: Our turn, our time.

MOIRA: *(To* PETER*)* You're disgusting.

HOARD: Friendly, I was going to cut you in on the pool—

FRIENDLY: All I need of that pool is right here, in my mind. *(Quietly)* Don't make me ask again.

PETER: Get out.

FRIENDLY: Peter!

PETER: You told him to get out. I don't want to look at him.

HOARD: There must be some mistake here.

PETER: No mistake old man. And take your drawings.

FRIENDLY: Sorry Hoard.

HOARD: Loyalty huh?

FRIENDLY: I don't have a choice here.

HOARD: (*Grabs* FRIENDLY *by the collar over the bar*) Thanks. You won't be so worried about your new clientele when I burn down this fucking bar—

PETER: Get off him—

(PETER *grabs* HOARD, *spinning him around and sending the playing cards everywhere.*)

FRIENDLY: Not in here—

HOARD: With one hand I'll whip a girl like you—

PETER: Get out.

(PETER *throws him towards the door.*)

HOARD: Come meet me—

PETER: Name it. (*Grabs the blueprints and wads them up, throwing them out the door.*)

HOARD: The pool. I'll be there.

(HOARD *exits.* PETER *lets out a war cry.* ISABELE *echoes it, then passes out again.*)

PETER: We won!

ISABELE: (*Momentarily lifting her head*) We won.

FRIENDLY: Goddamn Hoard.

PETER: You did the right thing—

FRIENDLY: I did what I had to do! Hoard's like family. We got history.

PETER: Oh, come on—

FRIENDLY: No. It's not that easy. *(Shaking his head)*
No. I'll be in the back, catching up on the books.
*(Reaches for a bottle, pours himself a shot of whiskey.
He downs it.)* Come get me if you need anything. *(Exits)*

NICO: Jesus.

MOIRA: Peter.

PRICE: Peter.

PETER: *(He turns to* MOIRA *and blanks. He has been so
caught up in the excitement he has forgotten for a moment
that* MOIRA *and* PRICE *are there.)* Oh—

MOIRA: Moira...I'm Moira. I don't recognize you...

PRICE: It's time to—

PETER: Between the two of you, I'm about to fucking kill
someone. THIS is me. Look at me. Did you see me
throw out Hoard? *(Silence)* What do you want? WHAT?
(She doesn't answer.) You want a kid? We are *young.*
Maybe that's how it works in Idaho. You want to be
parents? I thought you didn't even like your parents—

MOIRA: I never said that.

PETER: You always said that—

MOIRA: You've... You've never even asked about them.
They're my... parents. People that love me. That's what
you do, you love your parents. *(She starts to collect the
scattered playing cards off the floor.)*

PRICE: Why don't we just all calm down—

PETER: Don't tell me to calm down Price. You really
thought you were going to take me home? For *what.*

MOIRA: Peter—

PRICE: We both lost him Peter—

PETER: He was *my* brother. He was not *your* brother.
You need to move on or go back to your books.

God—she wants a family, you want—want what? Forgiveness?

MOIRA: Stop it.

PETER: What'd you do him man? Huh? Fucked with his head pretty good, didn't you. *(To* MOIRA *who is picking up cards from the floor)* Stop picking up those fucking cards!

PRICE: That was never the case—

PETER: I remember—how you were with him—*unnatural* Price.

PRICE: That's... Peter, I didn't...

PETER: He was sensitive. You knew that and you liked that. Never tried to help.

PRICE: *(Quietly)* I tried...

PETER: *(Laughing)* Did you?

PRICE: My life's work, from that point on—

PETER: He didn't get a life—

PRICE: What can I do? Peter whatever it is that will make you see, help you move on—

PETER: You don't get it. I'm here. This is The Now.

PRICE: I want us to know each other again, to be a fam—

PETER: You want family? *(Looking to* MOIRA*)* You? Alright. You be the mom—here we'll fashion a bonnet for you out of this cocktail napkin. I'll be the dad. Price...hmmmmm. Price you be our baby. Isn't he cute. Let's feed him and love him and take him places in the goddamn car. Wow. Look how he's growing—how fast they grow up. So fast. Birthday parties, baseball games. There he goes off to college. We are *so* happy. So proud. How can it be that he's already a young adult, twenty fucking years old. Isn't life *great*. Isn't this town swell. I

just whistle as I work. Wait. Wait—what's
happening—our boy! Our beautiful boy—he's —
(He grabs MOIRA *and* ISABELE's *mostly full drinks off
the bar and throws the first one in* PRICE's *face.)* Water—
so much water— *(Throws the second drink, drowning him
as if he is Michael)* Too much...too...much...fucking...
water. He's gone. *(Sits)* And it's over.

(Silence. MOIRA's *holding back a sob.)*

PETER: Why is it so quiet in here. The fucking jukebox
isn't even on. *(Walks over to the jukebox)*

PRICE: I see perhaps you're worse off than me.

(The phone starts ringing. After a few rings NICO *quietly
answers it.)*

NICO: Ship's Mast.

PRICE: I'll tell your mom I couldn't find you.

PETER: Tell her whatever you want.

(PRICE exits.)

NICO: *(On phone)* Uh-huh, I see...

MOIRA: Peter? *(Silence, he doesn't acknowledge her. She
tells the end of the Porthos story.)* The ocean at last, he'd
forgotten his past, just the buzz of wide open space.

(NICO, phone still to his ear, starts to listen to MOIRA's
*familiar story. He abandons the phone and he becomes
completely absorbed in it. During the telling,* PETER *shifts
and acknowledges, only for a moment, that this is the story
he loves.)*

MOIRA: The danger was near, and knowing no fear,
he fought with what seemed to be grace. In the razzle
and dazzle, the dance of the battle, the swiggle and
wiggle converge—

NICO: He dodges his rival—

MOIRA: His instinct survival, and thoughts of his river emerge.

NICO: His own destination, without hesitation, grabs fierce hold of his gut—

MOIRA: It quiets the swiggle, appeases the wiggle, and pulls him out of his rut. Without further adieu, he spins on a fin, he knows how to follow the call—

NICO: For to abandon it free is the trick of the sea—

MOIRA: But to return is the best trick of all. Peter?

(He does not turn.)

MOIRA: Peter—let's go West.

NICO: All that space!

MOIRA: Peter?

(PETER turns halfway toward her, hesitates, and turns back around. MOIRA waits for a moment then exits. NICO looks at PETER briefly, then exits after her.)

PETER: Bag of fucking rocks. *(He takes the marbles out of his pocket and chucks them out the door behind them, we hear them scatter on the street. He plays a song by Jolly Roger on the jukebox. He turns and sees ISABELE passed out on the bar. He walks over to her and slings her over his shoulder, his other arm raised in triumph as he exits.)* To the Pool!

END OF PLAY